Gallery Books
Editor Peter Fallon

MARINE CLOUD BRIGHTENING

Medbh McGuckian

MARINE CLOUD BRIGHTENING

Gallery Books

Marine Cloud Brightening
is first published
simultaneously in paperback
and in a clothbound edition
on 26 September 2019.

The Gallery Press
Loughcrew
Oldcastle
County Meath
Ireland

www.gallerypress.com

ISBN 978 1 91133 773 7 *paperback*
      978 1 91133 774 4 *clothbound*

A CIP catalogue record for this book
is available from the British Library.

Marine Cloud Brightening receives financial assistance
from the Arts Councils of Ireland.

Contents

for Pauline and Helen

After loving you so much
can I forget you for eternity
and have no other choice?
— Robert Lowell

PART ONE

Mariola with Angel Choir

In the shrill turquoise air
of first-century Palestine
the rough-hewn cross is already
regenerating: lily crucifix.

Jesus's lips are a winestock:
his Z-bend, the ropelike winding
of his legs are provocations
to the senses. He is smiling

almost as broadly as the pet
swan on his footrest — his keynote
above all is assurance —
bells and fragrances.

What strikes now is the sudden
glory of his smile in its measured
beauty, and the smiling
of his censing angels, an array

of thirty, bust-length,
jubilant and psalmodic,
great and trumpeting,
colossal and tremendous angels:

Angel with Crown of Thorns
(meaning whether herbs or harmonies
are capable of preventing
a demon from afflicting mankind),

Angel with Hawk, Lure and Gauntlets,
Angel with Bird of Prey, playing
a game with a hood, the frowning
Angel of the Expulsion.

Some slim and lithe, others
squat, one so fat as to seem
incapable of flight — one mighty angel,
the Angel of the Millstone.

Weighty, ample figures,
prodigious and surprising,
in their magnificent ranks
and zestful deviations.

In their *hilaritas*, their buoyant
musicality, their multiplicity,
their dazzling, swift and powerful
intelligences sharpening language

with their final vocabularies:
strong, resident angels,
vigilant, secreted angels,
imported to stand on colonettes

and crown the sacred kings of England;
greeting the precocious dawn
near the East window with its Northern
French geometry whereby one might

be seduced by it, and seduction
become rapture. (In summer especially,
the progressive illumination
during the dawn office of Lauds.)

The ninth order of angels, assuming
in their bustling jollity the wings
of the morning: still alert to this church
and its clumsy prayer, rotated

to their nimble and peculiar
fingertips, spectacular and outspread,
facing away in their strange idiom,
the spinning of the angels called Virtues.

Almost Lost Poem

to Polyphymnia — Muse of Legible Gesture

How can we say something new
with old words? Nothing is flatter
than words on a piece of paper,
gathered about one image
designed to injure the air.

The paleness of words
is a white pocket of shadow
that eats into the rest,
ghost-glimpses, an untying of knots
that persist after death.

The piercing rhythms of nature
sound together beneath the note
in poised wisps of meaning
taking them only from hope:
through the seasons of existence
weakened thought hushes.

And now the up-to-date world
with its core of worship believing badly
is something I could never have believed.

A past too close, that singular,
medieval autumn, reddening pictures
of fire and night, the notched
pear leaves, the botched resurrection.

Bleached, arrested, almost paralysed,
skies filled with water, the spreading darkness
just grazing Christ and flooding

on to His face's smooth features,
subject only to death.

He slakes his thirst on a jawbone
with slanting palm, his flesh as imperfect
as that quieted, crucified seraph
or six-winged angel, his large
brown wings now airborne.

The zigzagging, lit fold
strengthens the darks,
the angel's flattened hand projects
a halo-shape on the wall
above his head.

An expensive death, no sign,
the refusal of a tomb that can be visited,
and the faults of the departed, looped
over her hip, singly on her breast,
golden charity penetrates the window.

The Director of Sunlight

He painted this a hundred years ago,
a third son, mother a teacher of dance,
who met Saurin Elizabeth in a maritime parish,
a region untouched, sprinkled with white caps.
It is not an altar-piece of peasants adorning
luxurious walls but a 'Plage des Dames',
a corner, maybe of an orchard, of plums,
the garden in which he recovered from typhoid.

Exhibited as 'Lilies', or 'Lady with Trees',
it failed to sell, for its unrestful, decorative
qualites, its illusion too easily obtained.
For fifty years he was never to have a one-man show.
It could be 'Bean ag Léamh', 'Woman Reading',
or 'The Novice'. He had the bridal wear specially made,
for his bride-to-be, his mistress
in a nun's habit, yet to become divorced.

She wears a starched lace headdress
with a band around the front, peaked at the back.
Her gown looks flimsy under the wide sleeves
of the top wrap's pure ripples.
She has to endure her heavy stiffened
overskirt in intense heat, not raw sun,
but an even glow on her tanned neck,
her youthfulness.

To say how old she is, in the rich fertility
of that green moment, romantic figure
with forest depths all about it,
an encircled glade, an exceptionally balmy evening:
a girl called Space, who graced the rest
of my morning and is enough to carry me

to a new use of the mind, even if all
the supernatural stuff turns out to be wrong.

So why is he posing his favourite model
in a tinsel scarf, standing to the right,
framing her dark locks by her bonnet,
serenely in profile, or at prayer?
With her proud bearing and erect head
she seems to have just paused to incline her face
to the viewer in exquisite calm,
as of something passing, yet indelible.

He has eliminated the skyline, as if
he has cut a hedge down. You can see,
even in winter, the open mesh pattern
of the lace, the flower in the side of her hair.
She leans across as if listening
to unseen company, appears to grow
from the ground in a most perfect way
with a balance no plant could show.

Thin stems of fine leaves and half-shades
of cyclamen animate the instant,
set thickly in summer, almost hypnotically
awash with lavender, tall, upright, fully budded.
Petal heads curve like the strokes of grass
behind, mingle and absorb against
the sun-dried lawn, stripe against
the smoother grasses lying underneath.

Daisies thrusting in at the bottom
of the painting take up the mauve tone
in a simple arrangement, bathing
and winding through the yellow green.

He leads the eye through branches jutting
out and the sunlight which alights
to an enclosed background
of open airiness and conversational hedges:

a wild road where Sisters of the Holy Ghost,
formal in their pose and mood,
are following their quiet life,
their feet firmly rooted, but all
swinging round like the spokes
of a great wheel, detached by far
shadows in a cavelike effect. If scrutinized
too closely they would melt into darkness,

fingering their beads, their clothes flowing
in definition in the blur.
He sees them all as one and draws them
as a position of the earth.
We are not intruders, though part of a private
scene, a picture lovely to the sense
yet of a certain coldness, as though
she were already drifting out of view

with her questioning gaze momentarily
off guard or withdrawn, arrested,
trying to evolve her reflections — it is
possible she decorated the frame
before the failure of their seven-year marriage.
He said, 'It looks as if the Dublin people
have all the Leeches they want just now.
I would prefer to send you my nude

of the black woman, instead of that
blown-up watercolour in the National Gallery.'

Nevertheless it is interesting to contemplate
a 'tangled bank', however unorchestrated.
He fell off West Clandon railway bridge,
or let himself go, as the morning train
was pulling out in his direction
and lapsed into fitful sleep

where our so-called perpendicular lines
meet in the centre of the earth
like Mercury-women, in their Merry Widow
hats, on the mellow-splattered platform.
We all know the garden, the radiant
immortal garden, unfinished,
its burnt soil withered by the railroads
at each end of the same street

where every house reminds its neightbour,
I have been everywhere I was as a child.
It was such clearings in the wood of confusion
from which Paris scented itself with perfume
when, in August, lavender was cried
by the deadmongers' waggons
anxious to save time like bees
after the war burgeoned.

Bodhidharma Crossing the Blue River on a Reed

for Bob Welch

He was a moment in the conscience of humanity.

I may have feverettes, but I love
the utter halt of when it snows.
I am not, I will not be, leaping
to say, of course not, letting
my children grow up in my mind.

In a room that takes the place
of the mind a stair turns out
to be a door, given the direction
of time, and through the erupting
greenery the meadow is empty

of dog walkers. I change
how the character should sound
with ghastly trinkets. I have
no appetite for this metaphor
since the crack appeared in my life,

and a whole lost past went
through me, only by being worked
out to its end. If the eye
were an animal sight would be
its soul, or a more far-seeing

spirit. I believe at thirteen
you 'was' exactly Clarissa Harlowe;
over her left breast a little
pocket with an open flap
cast a dark triangular shadow.

Nothing melted away when he died,
not even, go, parasite, to the bloated
prison, his red hair covered with snow.
What he loved most in life
was radio broadcast, emanation,

present-day remnants of the creation
of the universe. The sea recedes
for the sake of the forest, the religious
afterpains of cannon are buried
under flowers. There are always

many worlds on earth, though officially
there are three, when you sense melted
glass, burned birds writhing, or lying
in my morning wrapper, brains
of nightingales, tongues of thrushes.

On the Sleeve, How Can Tears Dry in Two Colours?

for Caitríona, in memory of Emily

Opening an envelope of gloom
I am often tempted to organize
my small inner cemetery in such a way
that the sleeping shadows arise
and perform a dance
as child-size butterflies.

The only sound is the flick
of stiffened gauze and winglike vest,
a kind of negative halo around
their torn-off senses and ghost-hood.
Sometimes they mesh perfectly
with the angel who stands up inside them

and, hand to its lips, makes no attempt
to speak. If I may take the storm
to be one of words it was there
in the all-too-cluttered grave
that I learned how to sell my virginity
over and over again, to the heavenquake,

to place my hips directly in line
with his, who could so strikingly
withhold approval, his hand contracted
on my breast. Are you
the flower warden, or the spirit
of the iris, the white ghost

of the house on the left, half-child,
half-thrush, or a writing box
where a child's shroud lies pregnant

over the aborted material? In the untranquillity
of this ceaseless kitchen a person in yellow,
in a yellow prayer scarf,

with blue-clad fringes, is not content
to be timber and leaves of a ghost-
woman, from a rich new chapel
with pale purple floor, though
these colours are no longer considered
bright, by a season when outlines

are revealed. Cars are drowning
in the dew of the falling garden —
we think the hedges in stairs
that the winter must rust must outlive
us, imaginary flowers
will be able to play in the total

absence of leaves. The nettle garden,
the mist garden, garden for a day,
flows green in the suddenly black
state between two dreams. Like
a huge stage, the garden that light
writes is what lives on.

Elegy after Dennis O'Driscoll

He had been ten days dead when I heard it,
since Christmas Eve, and buried on New Year's Eve,
with his birthday following on New Year's Day.

No one thought to tell me except Tess;
perhaps they thought such news would break my heart.
My brother Dennis could die as suddenly,
in New Zealand, and I could not go.

Now there will be no more rave reviews
or birthday cards from 12 The Gallops
in the most fastidious italic copperplate
on the planet, or off it, or any other.

I ring Peter to ask for Julie's number
and from Tipperary spring the sweetest air
I know pours through my ear, saying, Dear,
forgive me for still being here.

A Handstitched Balloon

for Michael, in Ward One South

Arils of peace-engorged late moon freezing
on the water, then the late dawn whispering
on our breath: the changing tree-presence
time-deepens the orchardness of the tree-place,
and we love the veteran old trees for their ageing,
their orchard practice — high, honest capturers
and players of weather and light — working trees
and companion trees, even the closed canopy
they made out of larch trees.

A loose bellying north-south zigzag
rends and peels back the air
till the moon is not where it should be
and the earth elongates like a lemon.
The sounds of the taller trees are getting heavier
rather than lighter, the cider trees in the lee
of the hill show a thin branch of appleness
over the lane . . .

Countless journeys have made that path,
flow and flutter of limbs on a flowered
floor covering. And always in the wind,
the proximity of the sea, begrudging
in its beauty.

He had wanted to cut down all the trees
so he could collect stars from all over space
and climb up the telescope's steps with eyes
attuned to the dark crater thirty miles wide
on Venus. But some were missing, and others
recorded with the wrong brightness, up
on the roof of three adjoining houses

which divided the sky between them
so they could cover the entire night:

as each grave seems to have its companion tree,
when we consider a field,
as a stove can be disguised as a statue of love
and, in place of her breasts, two flowers.

Flying Fox

for David Hammond

Through old darkness and a streak of stars
behind the pebbled glass
we do not see the unilluminated doorway
where starlight survives its star.

If the eye were made of fire
sampling its coolness would tell us
how much of the darkening is due.

We do not stop to smell the odour-
lessness of the rhododendrons.
It's easy for the tree to measure
daylight's genuine touching.

The ice in the shadow beneath the leaf
is warmed by the leaf: the leaf
does not warm its shadow.

The air inside your shadow
weighs more than you do: your
shadow weighs nothing, nothing more

than this mirage of silence
slipping words
whose shadow lining gently changes shape

when two waves pass through each other unscathed
by the sound-shadow forming your head.

Living in the Airport

for Paul

Those early maiden days of the year
when the music is almost invisible
drifted news of you. I could see
the green shape of the garden
where we slanted our deckchairs
at the most luxurious angle.

The hounds of spring on winter's traces
caused an uproar in the newspapers;
with respect to the smallest brook
the readymade weather was bled
by otherworldly rounding out.

I was trying not to bump into anything
like an old neighbour who never went
beyond the landing. My passport
was a silver branch in a cream-wove
envelope scented from a rose of temperament
in the head of the sea.

The dazzling succession of the seasons
spread out their carpet of codes
like rehearsals for the hereafter
where this year's love wears horseskin moccasins.

Christ with his silence and his kiss.
One of his rings is of elephant hair
but the street does not show itself off
and we cannot arise and go there.

The Seed Mantra: A Gift Poem

Sweeping up a leaf
that blew in last November
I thought, there will be no more
autumns, I shall have no more winter
this year, I thought it best
to omit the season.

I went out in a fiery field
to find a propitious name
for a child in the four
afterlife realms, and something
was bestowed, a plaited blonde
wave-shape in faded yellow.

Yet everything was white,
the textile handles with ribbons.
The double line of gold
around the dust of some,
the scythes cutting through the pearl
of this year's sequence of wet and fine.

Landscape with Cannon

The miracle has happened:
we were the army that never was,
the generation that was allowed
to live; the part of the animal
fed to the hounds that have
run it to ground.

Flowers without stamens,
some parched, some underripe,
with large metal buckles
just below our knees, drab dresses
and bashed-up hats.

Everybody was staying in their
homes in case they found themselves
in a traffic-snarl at the hated
Customs wall. The city was like
a lump in one's throat,

with its bombs and its prayer music.
A city where killing was easy
and the cheapness of life at the time
had an increasingly faded elegance,
though some people sat casually
on the ground, in the carefully demarcated zones.

We were living in someone else's city,
port of mists and edginess,
hence, my ingrained gloominess,
the angle of my soul gradually
losing its grip on the exact depth

of the wounds. He directed the hunt
from the beginning with steely gaze,

bellowing voice charged with anger
and spite — having struck a crucifix
with a sword, taken two hosts

and placed them carnally inside
a girl in green peril. Days
of public rejoicing turned to sugar
riots, soap riots, official delirium
in deserted, snaking streets,

parallel gatherings on prepaid nights.
I'd give you half my remaining years
to explain life in the north,
its dusky seventh, the end
of me, the real end.

He has his whole life spread out
before him and is obviously dying,
scrolling through thoughts rising higher
than his breath. The iron band
around my heart loosens.

How will things be in ten years' time
when every day is a decade
and ten years now is like two thousand years,
in the garden of equality with its chic
cafés? Winter, we gather.

We learn fresh languages for dead
leaves on at least forty streets.
One had one's back to the peace monument.
The bomb is probably lodged in there
where it will be safe from bombs.

PART TWO

in memory of Seamus Heaney

A Pauline Verse

for Onesimus

I warned Paul, now that we know
the latest half-rhyme for dear Seamus,
wasps, leaves and berries at Lammas,
the twittering of gathered swallows,

I would twitter all his name means,
the golden means in what was his name,
from ah to Amen, amass and âme,
amuse and Amy. From ash to Ashe

and ashes to ashen, assume to aum.
From ease to easy, eheu and emu.
From ham to hay to hey to hen,
from he to hue to hum, human

and Hume. From hymn to hymen,
no less. From eyes to Enya.
From mane to manse to may
to May and many, from my

to mash and mesh and mush,
meas and Mass, mensa, mens
sana, Manus, mess and messy.
Muse ever. From nay to neem,

to Nessa, same to sane to say
and seam, Sean, seem and seen,
see and semen, sea and shy,
shun, shame, sense, sans and seamy.

From snámh to sauna, she to sheen
to Sheena, Shauna, Sue to Susan, Susie.

From sum to sun, us to use, yea to yeah,
yeah, yeah. From yam to yes and yum:

from hem to Esmé, suas
to anuas. From Una to Esau
to Aeneas. From hussy to he-man,
from me to Shaman.

Night Journey of the Solar Bark

It feels to me like an oblique place.
The earth hath been iron in this land
and the heavens brass this summer:
a fall of all the back hair
links me to the skin of his heart.

It is changing but it is not us,
the place where we once were children,
that small part of the world where we
were formerly at home: they bury him
in the soil from which he has sprung.

There were door to door movements,
the space headway, time headway
of the speed-sensitive articulated lorry,
my shallower landward rhythms in the bus lane,
my dwell times at a station stop.

My journey was much less tidal
than the earthquake in the South
with the wan sky bending its nocturnal
unhinged rainbow in the sunless light,
lemony moment as pale as silver.

Blotches of doomed yellow streak
the ancient ice in a zone of stones
that may or may not be a cemetery.
A few more carefully chosen handholds
and he will boost himself over the lip

of the rocks, thrusting, as he does so,
the small twigs inward. Where and what
is this sandy path between the shingle
and the dune? His negation of behaving,
struck midair and driven downward

like the shuttlecock in badminton.
I am cruel in putting it this way, but it is true,
sweet leftover, sweet sealed disabled lips.
Little prepares us for your glassy
ironic remove, the two or three

words of lead that dropped so deep
and keep weighing. Rapturous, strange
death that got the world afloat
and the climate weirding to a four-degree,
the drinking of two exquisite wines at once.

How I miss your written voice,
your throaty measures quoting
from the intense reds in the sky now
whether the joining of your hands
will be sacred. The passage is not really

mysterious, occurs at a lull
in the skeletal motion, where he is at his most
sepulchrally supernatural. The upper voices
go their own way — the dead have been disturbed
by *une mort très douce*, by a strong

walk-up window. All attempts
to fear with or for him are cut short
by this too crowded elsewhere, this inaccessible
peace, the re-enwombing, after
there is a North, of the untroubled petal.

Unmade Silks

Now the pageant and effort of his life
are laid before us, as he retreats
into the literary hinterland,
I have the right to stay quiet in my corner.

His life was lighter but also darker,
he churned what it is to be human,
to unsee the other city, the woman's
moist eyes. But something about

the low sill when one is sitting
means the window as a filter is lost,
the ceiling void, the room is crossed
with light from the reputed bed.

The Light Well

Greetings, my dear ghost, spectral husband,
we have our embrace,
the windows fidget at their fastenings
with every plunge and suck of the sky.

The season of letter writing is over
for us, when white roses tapped
at the evening-prolonged window —
the presence of black violets

on the bridal bed counterpane,
on the charm quilt, where each fabric
is used only once, was a little more
overripe than the smell of wreaths

in the hall. It always seemed to me
it would be 30,000 years until
you died, as if you were my Eurydice
whose wizard lips and firethought are closed.

Even as it narrows over time
on the inside, life moves progressively
deeper into the corners, dressing up
the future, while the heart sprays off

into dust, as Shelley's silk-
wrapped heart enfolded
in pages of 'Adonais'.
Or take the pen from his hand

and leave him sleeping at his desk
like a crow quill in a prayer pocket,
my spirit will all the same
lay itself down next to you.

Three Bibles of Light

We go to a wedding: her dress,
when you saw it, stirred you,
thin fire racing underskin,
nor desire into the aftertime.

I keep forgetting he's dead
for a millisecond at a time,
mad ghost train out of control
to look upon the dewy lotus banks

of Acheron. Year without summer.
The weather is in motion, seems actual,
moors, rooms, orchards, deserts, red thunder,
why keep watching?

As if with a very difficult sister —
what is there to see? No thou,
touching my left hand to his lips,
as though it weren't really a night of time.

He may, as the prophet says, tarry.
But what kind of witness would that be?
Earth will be warmer than we thought,
with the autumn of his body —

the silver fell in dust from the roof
on to our plates, first with yellow flame,
later with blue. My co-wife's spirit
husband like some organ of the moon

in the late civil twilight's sky quality.
The yellow-brown colour of the moon,
the fullest moon we'll ever see.
In a way you have torn the water,

you could send signals through gold
just as waves are bent as they pass
around an island. They remove more light
than their shadow may suggest.

The column of falling rain is altered
by its trip over the tannin-laced
swamps. Even if the light is totally smeared
out in the non-blue mirror eyes

and though we remain incurious about
the nature of his passing, known to the unknown,
or the grievability of his life,
this morning had just such a sky.

The Cemetery for the Ashes of Thought

Today I experienced these rooms above the trees
as love in the form of ghosts. The spirit begins to dress
you, master of cheerful knowledge. At least
four generations nourished themselves on his thought.

His footsteps were as decisive as the breeze
from an opening is the pause from which to enter
the zigzag house, even the way a priest goes
up to his pulpit, within the church bell's limits.

The place was born again when they poured
the wall and reworked the opening.
Instant light everywhere remains the old light,
you might say the horizon is everywhere

as the city is alive, cold museum, treasury
of shadows. At that time we lost the horizon
as we are about to lose the earth which embraces
one's body so we cannot escape.

Whatever was blown or carried into the space
the passage is dim and private,
nothing to add or take away.
You sleep on a table, the waterfall rushes

freely under you, lying completely imprisoned
in a box on the earth's crust, a lid
offering protection, though I got very little
help from a thankless comet.

You journey under the horizon
like an in-between figure who tries to establish
a dialogue: great comforter that lies there
breathing, like a child that shouldn't freeze.

Darkness gains a new importance
when fire invents a room or a house contains
night's light — the house is constantly giving
darkness to the fire's computerized flame.

Its wandering in time is strong enough
to say, come, live inside me
by a less-used door: the arms
of the cross transform around its core.

But the core is not dissolved
with your inner thoughts, your now slowed
decay erasing the ways you might
move from one horizon to another.

Gold Toad

The one able to say vanishes
like a train uncoupled from its engine
or a sort of mystical body
alongside the real body,

body exposed to weather and caress
on the earth's dreamy crust,
the soul of half the country
for more than half a century.

Someone is before us in the tree
and on the ground, someone has soaked
into the ground — where else could we turn,
to the anonymous rustling?

The reversibility of the flesh
into walls of stone and clay?
Will you be able to keep coming forth
from the place we have not yet learned

to find a voice for? Windswept hair,
whispering voice, authoritative
and self-effacing, avuncular and aloof,
of our 'national treasure'.

A glance was ignited
by the breath of my glance:
seeing into one's own nature
freed nature from its spell.

Submerged by the night,
he is closed in over upon himself,
sensing the sensation of unmediated
contact with the elements.

And the powerlessness of that singular
face, the frailty of the one who is counting
on you, is like the loss of the stunning gold
toad with its green and travelled Virtues.

The Unwatched Life

A sea of wheat flows in the simple fields
as if the city has changed its mind offshore.
The ribbon window in the remains
is a blue stripe along the body
that can be turned off at night.

The old aquatic eye has been lost
but in some sense the sedentary clam
is still seeing, in the world of what would
ordinarily be called seeing,
though no eye movements can be seen.

Such eyes make no sense, and seem
to break all the rules, stained spots
steering the head as it swims
to coarse landmarks, cup eyes,
pit eyes, with slits notched in the pupils.

Others have eyes sprinkled all over
their backs, or eyes at the tips
of their arms. The double eyes
of the spookfish look through a fog
like the headlamps of a large car.

It cruises with half its eye above
and half below the equator, self-luminous
as the nipples covering the butterfly's eyes
whose colours disappear after the unsilvered tail
is buried in mud like the ark.

Noah's Ark for Seeds

The forest has been plotting this moment.
The uneventful days have begun.
Our earlier handwringing is riddled with thought
like any old table leg with worms.

By the clock of the long now
June can be read like January.
We look in the moon which represents
our two seasons and are dry in soul
since he last walked the earth.

After the murderous nibbling away of the winter
he is covered in a skein of sensitivity,
the manes of the clouds slowly seething
around a pear-shaped hill,
not like rushes around water.

His sleep scanty and disturbed,
he continued to tremble for a fortnight
in his race to toxicity and deaf ears.

His exposed flanks have no shadow,
the swelling wound of his heart
cools down to a thin, sharp pain.

And everybody tells surface-water things
as he is pulling the horizon to him
to free the bricked-in streams.

The flavour would still be bright
had we known tomorrow
one of the poems thrown into his grave.

The O'hEighnaigh

Salt is invisible, the true opposite of decay,
white gold for de-icing roads.
The flower of salt from the salt pool,
the salt lagoon, is white and purple as the heather
daisy. Whenever wood is used
in its making, salt is dark.

At that time, dear Lily, there wasn't much
of maybe. They couldn't build the church
out of anything *but* wood. His mouth
was set in a kind of difficult beauty:
one describes his face as stony, another
refers to granite, others prefer the word
craggy, as a litho-landscape.

He was astute, shrewd and fluid, a good man
in a boat; an accurate hammer of a man,
a man for the shovel and loy and warrior deed
of his tongue-twisted history.
He was generous in the meadhouse
where the dark slender boy retains the upper hand.

A man before his time, a man after
his time. Upwardly mobile, he was a throwback
in suit and shined shoes,
a cleaned-up noble savage, so to speak,
some said . . .

He spent a spell learning English,
as long again without an ounce of sense,
but that's enough about that.
Thinking in Irish, while writing the story
in English, he could say things without
telling them, in the fossilized treaty

language, emotionally enmeshed
in the local, in his kinship ties,
in family and friends by the open hearth,
the bellows and turf, the half-door and settle,
the milk churns, the flagstones and fiddle
where they lilted for someone to jig.

He spoke bluntly about the hard times,
losing his brogue when he left home
from shanty to curtain as heroes always do.
He was not particularly reverent
but implicitly understood the contradictions,
played with them, creating a whole series
of personae that continue to evolve.

His melodic tunes had the snappishness
of a dog. And though no one really wanted to return
he allowed us access to the donkey cart
and the creels. Meet me in somewhere,
gatekeeper guide, spectre at the feast —
i láthair Dé go rabhad ag rince,
in the presence of God may he reel.

The By-catch

He delves back into transoceanic memory,
a sea that concentrates, a sea that explodes.
I embark upon the tide of his sleep,
polluting the event with doubt.

His fragments are not decayed, but strong:
when would it stop, the echo in the throat,
when would he enter that light?
A sleeping man with an angel behind him.

You hear me with eyes alone,
seeing everything from nowhere,
striving like earth's shadow to reach the moon.
Now he is a weary adult, now a young boy.

It was as a trembling puppet that I saw him,
his potential to crumble with the next turn
of the kaleidoscope. Body in which silence
resonates as if it were sound — the importance

of the diminishing sounds — little by little
let him attain to quietude, let him not
think of anything, not of his paintings
that have hung on no wall.

We are already living translated lives:
when I try to raise my eyes to your face
fire breaks out, not because you were warding
me off. The loss keeps us to our path,

it tears the mouth wide open,
the mouth that had once talked to me,
your ins and outs after reaching dead ends.
Your index finger is glittering in the air,

the fist pulled back like a nutcracker
trying to hold the nut. Words simply
lead to other words and so, if autumn,
then true, the frailty of the faithful.

The sentences disappear into the daylight
at the exit. I am standing behind you,
your neck bared, you don't feel
my lips with your dumbed-down,

over-delicate skin. But can you hear,
cell by rain-washed cell,
the cobwebs and moontalk
of the unlocker of doors?

Tree Portrait Taken at Dusk

Blessèd is he who left the banquet
of life without drinking all the wine
in the glass — who didn't read his novel
to the end and was able to bid it farewell

at once. Pencils still lie
on the illuminated table in his room
as if it were just another working day.
He rested quietly, a corpse

in sultry weather, but he was new
to death and looked as if he might
get up and go about his business:
there was a small black hole in his temple.

His hands with their fingers upcurled
seemed to have no connection to the rest
of him. To see with the mind this deep
opening, to think with the eye his neglected

grave that houses out of the as-found
something that has not yet arrived.
To speak of the ghost and indeed to
and with it, beneath the undamaged

chestnut trees, in the cemetery,
'In Paradisum', the built-in dappled
shadows, the sage and peach silks
of the garden, winter cherry and the dead

leaf colour. We actually realize
how low the level of the ground is,
that is how it has been up to now;
everything is there waiting for us.

Dark marks on the white bark.
The perfect silver edge of that
magnetic balcony looking out
over nothing, shot through with unprecedented

dazzling figures. Neither the wind
in the opened up city nor the leaf interest
can make the city meaningful.
Nor the fact that the path keeps

going till a tongue of the inside
floor tastes clean sharp sand
or first snow. The resurrection
is not a door that exactly opens easily,

unless for Saint Rita, patron of
the impossible. Death is possible
for everyone, more than being born
or hearsay of it. How trees lift

water to great heights.
There will be an empty
setting at the already
laid table: it is his.

To the Source Person

Death was your final gift to life,
not a hymn to extinction.
The black earth appears on the surface,
the deeper ground promises the earth.

Part of it is decaying, part nascent,
like opening up a new heart
darkened to elephant grey —
have the places left you along with me?

The horns of the moon have met four times
since I lay with you upon beech fronds,
trying to fall out of love. Beeches
inscribed by you preserve my name

into the anonymous murmur, the cup-marked
stone whose eyes can never be met.
Some women have horse shadows
since words deserted you

like a city without a park. If you
could roam London as an aerial spirit
the gossamer roof of the museum
would look for your story.

There are compressions and explosions of space
as the underground people we knew
take up the world-work,
sleep downstairs on the window sills.

Transmission of the Letter 'S'

I find no sleep in my sleep,
that there is no such thing as silence
or darkness, to willingly dissolve.
If anything nature is all over,
the actions of the wind unleashing
the sun on earth as though rivers
had never existed before.

The gossamer sounds of rainbow bombs,
church bells with wet ropes, the trembling,
unlistenable city continuously ringing
old sunlight from the thinner sky there.
Its original churning surfaces end in white.
The thawing sand yet red with day
like Jupiter bursting the eye to the eye.

The stars calm down despite body glimmer
while the smeared sound in question is like
blurred lilies, a departing lover, because
our only nest is our wings. Dwellings below
and fields upstairs for stars and their absences,
each roof is planted to become
another level of the garden.

We still do not know how much less nothing
can be, listening to the lightning that tempts
the sky, singeing the dead air, the predicament
of its texture. Clouds can feel the work
and, plus or minus, the past will be reshaped
by a nostalgia for the present. I was myself
and held my petulant garb.

Such a mechanical wife. The angel spirit
goes from one side of the spiritual bedroom

to the other, reworking every deadline,
thwarting every repetition. Then he came
with his old proverb and I understood
he had nothing left to say, no words rushing
against words, one wrapped into another.

The river of the dancing meadow
of keeping is open, continuance
of a perpetual waxlight, woman plus house.
People could be heard communicating
underground, slight swellings to a scenting
dog. The probable castle just rising
up by the unenclosed souterrain.

I must desire you, give me leave,
in spring all trees become pregnant,
this spring as you wrote it might be
in a poem called 'Magdalene Facts'
addressed to her reflection. The dream
had no sense of war, to photograph
the clearest veins of angel air.

PART THREE

Marine Cloud Brightening

Of all our painful ghosts
she held her breasts like stranded energy,
perhaps containing secrets
in the tranquillizing chair.

Your own grieving was put on hold
in pockets of rescue, the red stain
that depicts her cheek,
the carelessly folded tea towel,

the cut-glass voice of someone handing you
something hidden in flowers.
When wells go cloudy
it is safe to assume that clouds

are there for a reason, painting
the newly dark mountains.
There may be weather wars
as we weaponize the weather,

its whiter daytime skies,
its redder sunsets. Others are stealing
our rain, turning down the sunlight
with an umbrella hanging low

over the ash-dimmed earth
where all weather occurs.
If this light is invisible to us
why do we need it?

The sky could be rendered
discernibly bluer by that
library of shadows
lurching the liner.

Cloud Chamber Photograph

Lusitania — missing — a baby girl, age 15 months with fair curls and rosy cheeks, in white woollen jersey and leggings, tries to walk and talk. Send any information to Miss Browne, Queen's House, Queenstown.

I polish the sky which heaven dilates
with a single stray hair from the Greek
word for sea. My years have their own
language, talking about the time
all the time.

Her first full day at sea, after the tugs
at last backed her out into the Hudson,
she carried twenty trainloads of coal
for the single crossing, 65,000 gallons
of engine-cooling water for every journey.

She could not have steered a more perfect
course. Sycamore and satinwood, her internal
pathway almost followed the wood pores,
from south to north meaning. The lightning
mappers picked up messages of thunderdays,

of thunderstorm days, of thunderstorm rainwater,
two charged thunderclouds, their feet close
together, their airglow layer soft hail
in the virgin air right up in the eyes
of the ship, cloud flash and lightning crouch.

How fast the field is moving,
he wrote to his Aunt Josephine,
with his grocer's assistant's mind.
The lifetimes of the signatures
were low, not rain, not leaves.

In daydreams of nest-engracing nature,
I was wondering what my own eyes
would look like, chipped open
by the resilient corals bleaching white
under stress, laying down skeletons

from sudden towers of life, corals pale
as ghosts gliding, all the while
fighting off seagulls. A broom handle
in the wake, then two white streaks
running along her name in gold letters

on her bows like an invisible hand.
Flashover in wet woods, skin breakdown
above the melting point of brass
or copper-skinned brass buttons
that the gas turned mouldy green.

Major Pearl flung up a gold-braided arm
like a black searchlight that would block
out the moon. The electrical insult
had sprained her left wing, the long
spark confused the bright foam

with the clear water, till the ocean
became bare within eighteen minutes.
Except for the fishing boat *Bluebell*,
fitting the horses' hooves with mini-sandbags
and gas masks like a fine necklace.

Sabbath Morning, 8 O'Clock

The street comes true,
the self-praise of the lapwing's
speech is established for the bird
at each dawn.

Only time comes along
for these fallen future fathers.
The silky glare of an enhanced light
shares memories with matter

all the way back
to the mean number of rain days.
The full prying apart
of the end of history or some such thing

arches up the earth
like more than a billion horses
which have roared towards the tightest
thread being stretched.

Deception Island

They get into meditative states easily
but you cannot make pets of them
ransacking the oceans standing in a bobbing
zodiac. It takes moon palms and wet courage
to break through to, to break a porpoise,
to drive a dead dolphin in a Prussian attack.
Those sudden room-sized breaths
cured the white paint on the ships
to a haggard parchment, stained an ovary
lilac from the grey whale's frolic.

PART FOUR

Unrequited Love for the Weather

How far gone the summer is!
Some brown is returning, my yellow has faded
like a handwriting that has lost its hand
(I don't want thee to word my letter,
I only want thee to write it).

How early autumn came this year,
she would say, loudly, and burn the paper,
those perused love letters. Everything she recalls
happened in that library, whose books
have their spine cut into with a razor.

One does not think thoughts, one thinks
the forming of words, the times, thank God,
are over, my past without thoughts.
I began to perceive, to gain
some here and now transcendence.

My life was a collection of future reminiscences,
a continuous yesterday ahead of time,
and all that geography was within me
spending all day under the British flags,
whatever shape they are, nipping the island in two.

You could go swarming off
into the television space
where war flows from the screen
and this handmade world becomes fuller
and fuller. To dream of a church is prison.

Misfortunes accustom you to superstition,
but what does that prove, I thought.
The sky itself was beginning to think,

the ingredients of our days, the larger
shadows, the lime-white glamorous clouds.

The filmed-over sun would fire by itself
in my pocket, as if going up a ladder.
I woke up several times in the night
from poisoned joy, such ringing of the doorbell,
such layering of wives crawled up to me

and made no sense at all.
She is in paper-frail health and seeks
to lash out against the tongueless bell,
to cloud a few slim bones
with last breaths caught in silver

while my father would struggle to throw
some heavy rope across the roof,
and I would have become the colour
of a raincloud, invisible as rain,
as the hair in the notebook,

the sleep-pin that is in her hair.
Then he would promptly wrap
his fingers into a denial, since
the beautiful things did not adorn
the room — no lace, no television set.

Yet at that time I was a person
with different honey seasons
as honey ripened like a diary for two
in this most undiarylike of times,
and my prayerful body was a smear

of rain that glowed freer
than among my haunted furniture.
Where did you find those ghosts?
In the ponds, in the ceremonial
re-hanging of the curtains?

How the Angel Began to be Proud

In her first dream she gazes up
to where his face should be.
There is nothing contained
about the use of red on the mouth,
the blood-red cocoon for the body.

She envisages thought as if it were
trembling in her ankles, a manufactured
not-knowing who manages the angel,
the father of the angel? Why should time
seem to stop here,

where the sea is sunk deeply
into itself, and the scalp has been
re-sewn with wire, beyond the closest
world? Everything was quiet, dry
and urgent, though that eye will be wet.

In a world completely knotted
together, born things are re-born,
gathered back through the inward
bruise of the beyond, with silence
at the wrong times, and speakings at the wrong times.

For then there will be a willing
and there will be festivals.
I too have dawns around me, none
of them printed, his green-violet
veins, his white-pleated robe.

The Decision to Kill John

John had been a problem since 1927
when he ripped open his trainer:
he rattled the thick chain on his legs,
swayed back and forth in the elephant house.

Since the multiple gunshots would cause
a commotion his access to food and water
was stopped for seventeen days
while twenty-two other companions were poisoned,

strangled or stabbed to death.
The team had begun bringing
the necessary chemicals and tools
to preserve his elegant hide.

The dissection took four hours;
his skull and brain are preserved
in a large jar in the university lab.
His lethal tusks were torn off and weighed.

His flesh and bones were hacked
and deposited in a hole dug
in front of the concrete monument
to Tokyo's deceased animals.

He had fallen and struggled to his feet
repeatedly. The hide was donated
to the Imperial Army in hope that it might
be used for soldiers' uniforms.

The Shape of This How

The May litany is chanted
in the misty twilight edges of the fields.
They are lighting candles at cemeteries,
priests are whispering.

The village name means 'frostbite',
also 'cuckoo bird'. There was a soldier's city
somewhere on the outskirts of town
past Apple, Pear and Plum Streets

where everything was washed away
and the earth was so intelligent
as not to resist the birth
of the new personality.

We rubbed our cloth shoes with chalk
until they were shining white.
He would observe the weather through
the window, complained only to his diary.

Amid all the useless chatter,
to name one's child 'Belfast',
I sprinkled some unborn poems
over my forest brother's pestered head,

mussing his hair, kneading his knees,
sprayed with holy water.
Such a molten state of mind —
I grew up under his wing.

And now you will see
the frightened shadow of a cloud
scurrying across the sublime
pastoralism of his late poetry.

The poems approach us like a tawny
iceberg. Take the sheepskin
off your soul, watch
the coming and going of ships,

dream peacefully
under chestnut trees,
rest in the silvery sand
of the riverbank.

Inside a Slashed Tennis Ball

Ten times a day we thought we had emptied
the reservoir of misery. Beneath his eyelids
his eyes kept as firm as horn or iron or the blood plum.

Six glims around his trap-case, the plastic ID
bracelet still on his wrist, hoping some other
might come who perished long ago,

the name spray-painted on the rear window.
It does not go anywhere in particular, it simply
goes on. Even in the incense-stained atmosphere

of this suburb of heaven you hear things that are far
and near, people making love. She finds in every season,
perhaps in everything, thunderstorms about her brother,

stops and frisks, just the ordinary God. I do not ask
to see the distant scene, the dark-fanged hand-shaped
rose melted on the silver-threaded chair: for fear

of crushing a unique moth or orchid,
or the above mentioned aware.

Promises of Routes

Two days' worth of weather
leaves a dusk over everything,
a mountain of brown clothing
like a protective shroud.

The kerb ended
as we wandered down the yellow-
brown avenue, to enjoy every tint
of the winter olive harvest,

nor was I once bored
or wished it to stop.
Had we not gone our ways?
Who he saw, where he lived even,

had long been lost to me.
He has grown large
but still has the angular twisting
movement of a thin man.

His face is moon-shaped, pink-brown.
It used to be lank and cadaverous,
a little frieze of very fine
hair at the back of his head.

Lines more marked, skin
less plumped out, rather shrunk,
sunk cheeks, always burning,
paunch as round as a marble.

White and shaky, charcoal
black around his eyes grows
vague. He likes to be
listened to and chatters on,

then lies back in the armchair
like an animal in a trap,
perpetually looking at the time,
drinking, smoking, then says

he couldn't sleep. Crushed
in the head, he cannot walk
without pain, his great
joints seem to crack.

Alone, he falls into trances,
comas, wants innumerable
blankets on his bed,
innumerable cups of tea.

Making strange faces,
suddenly hooting with laughter,
cramp in the muscle of his heart,
his toes curl up.

It is only a question
of treatment, I have to
give him claret and sit by him,
spinning party talk

about carpentering and bulbs,
anything to keep talking,
inventing, distracting.
What's the use of looking ahead?

Alas,
he carries off the years
as if he were
drumming slightly in the veins

who stalks beside me in many
different shapes. The summer
is in his brain, driven
like a motor in the head,

his head swaying like
a captive balloon. He was like
a spine to me, I take
my own brain out

this fine September morning
when it may be August 3rd,
1914. Not that I ever
think of him as dead,

the breath pressed out of him,
but keep the soul:
no one so illuminated,
I will go on doggedly

until I meet him myself.
I always notice the weather
in which people die . . .
One has dreamt away

the fact of his death,
to which I woke —
I went up and dressed his bed,
the blinding whiteness of his bed.

Playing Ghost with Julie

As long as heads stay bowed
it was he had a life
the way the dark changes
you as you always were.

He thinks he will never want
that time back, slips somehow
into the locked church, the first
frosty flowerbed, first woods

and second woods. His voice
touches the soft summeriness
to go into the bone. The light
goes off on his voice, since all voice

comes from the end. But as long
as the words go on in the present,
as were we still, we are enfolded
in someone else's voice, in the brighter

darkness. The past often regards itself
as poetry, the heart racing faster
through the afternoon, like charity
in summer, the white feeling

of glimpses of the moon. Am I
as much as being seen, as big
as a minute, watched by still
deeper eyes or the futile harbours

of what is not yet? There are
deepenings, satiny movement
and depth, some sea-state
a reminder of dessicated gardens.

The earth has buried his arms
as rings turn pale when a beloved
is in trouble. A song has stopped
things in their course

and the warm dream is cut through,
all gone from mind, or what she calls
her mind, slight though it is.
There was no dream to blame

for needing to wake up so often
and drift into dreams so many times.
What has thought to do
with time and space, does water

dissolve thoughts, do thoughts drown
in this immensity of strangely
mental water? With a last flutter
thought settles on its perch

and goes quiet as it sounded
in the moment. I removed the not
from the never not there breath
like comforting butterflies arising

naturally — like blue eyes,
or cells when stained by the inspired air,
the wintry air after a heavy dinner,
the flower hospital where all is prayer.

The Laboratory of Grace

Tortured, afflicted, pined, consumed,
wasted, tormented, they lay in their swoons,
their ears heavy like the deaf adder
to charming never so wisely.

But if all should singly pass before me
into a state of perfect nothing
it would be what grace felt like
carried with it, filtered through

the farthest reaches of the melting hymn.
There is no infallible sign of grace
but grace marrying grace,
the scene shifting in the theatre,

the warming effects of summer flowers.
Angels have had about 5,000 years'
experience, they are full of eyes
behind and before that ascension

of our parable. His intense
and passionate breathings were incivilities
within the light which lucid spirits
collected in the bottom of his eye.

That eye became a host for the oversoul,
a lens detached from its heart-pocket
embedded at the top of the wigwam
within the book of John.

The Pardon Churchyard

It is snowing gossamer
undecayingly
on all the cavities created through death.

There have been forty days
of true pardon
since the pre-beginning and the post-end.

The dark dove,
the dark light,
the after sight.

The copper river was dreaming
of crystal ships
and a hand shadowed with solar roses

tasted poison every day
from tulips and chimneys
and thus managed to last.

Perhaps put two summers together
like a mender of nets
linking silver charms on a silver loop

only after he has ritually washed the rope,
between his inner and outer skin
to shine to the very last second

of lowering sun. The light was not received
by so obvious anchors
as the flat plate of cloud

and the not quite parallel churches.
Strong and of a family,
a true peasant,

there must be one fearless
but rather dangerous person
destructive most of all to themselves.

He's standing, drinking Scotch,
close to the swimming pool,
and thirty years have passed

since a wrongful birth to you and Mary,
himself and his uncle's wife.
You only blame me as you did

from that first day.
Here was my sister, father, brother,
son, all that I had.

This is my son and while there's life
in him he's half mine.
Take your half, or that silence for it,

a rain-blessed island of consumptive
cousins, as if the blue colour
of my soul brother were hidden in the yellow.

Their breathing is out of step
with the beckoning roof,
and the cold coming in under the door sill.

A suddenly legible heart
keeps watch over the river
where earth took earth from the earth

like a long skyview let into the city
that cannot make meaningful
the city pulled apart.

One apparently simple
and undeveloped
but liable to show unexpected magnitude,

unexpected power, passes into the leaves
on the branches and the air
between them. He becomes

too rebellious, in which case
he may have been misconceived
at the start, and he's trying . . .

This fruit shall hang very still,
one that brushes away the earth
with its marble casing.

Who can tell, in an emptied world,
the narrowest thread, the nautical
rope, the strand of DNA

in his calcified backward twist
and always burning swallows?
The past cannot be held in place

between his parted teeth.
So one of the sort-of-dead,
or newly dead,

is spirited away to the scaffold
of heaven, and cautiously
resurrected

as in all past Januaries,
a tongue of the inside door
tasting the first snow.

Encounters with Dust

I avoid books about the present or last war,
the war has never been. The air
is thinning itself for the breakup of winter.
Breadths of breeze-requiring sun
slice through any and every complaint
to a dark kind of summer.
Moon scuffed at its edges, brighter,
narrower, smears its self-improvement mirror-
image of giveaway light into the rich world
at the basement of Europe.

A dull church bell in a parody of greeting
uses all the languages of the body
to revamp your soul and get that space
between your thoughts. The day may be
about your spirit, she chimes in with a ribbon
of praise in your daily gratitude journal,
you find a little spiritual intervention
in your electronic in-box via Skype,
morsels of frenzy and balm, from those
electronic churches, before hitting the treadmill.

Remembering the voices that used to fly ahead
I should have kept both voices alive
in my mouth where shadows fester.
We saw the pale dove-grey coffin,
overgrown like a stage coffin,
go down step by step into the well.
Like hearing the rain in hotels, we dropped
the primroses in at the bottom of a steep,
brazen grave laid like an old rose,
surrounded by black and white butterflies.

Roses lit like lamps burnt yesterday
with a bunch of our red and white carnations on top
of it. Its very long after afterglows
glazed some flicker of the snowdrop
pallor into the next lap of the year.
There is no way we can make the eyes
of the blond Christ on his slim cross
look at us, wrists twinkling with diamonds.
And now some sachet of holy dust
sets my book alight in another field.

Fragment of a Litany

Uncentering city-cut moods
jigsaw together.
Splashes of oneself are glisteningly
available
as carcasses of worn-out vessels
scourging the same urgent line
on the water. A series
of pre-existences that grew up sheltered
are tokens of nests-to-be.

The expected blanket of night
sounds blunt. Leechdoms, wortcunning
and starcraft trim the skyline.
Paired saints press against buildings
at walking speed
whose walls if allowed to alter
by the consideration of simples
would be holding a very different
book.

Acknowledgements

'The Director of Sunlight', a response to 'A Convent Garden, Brittany, c.1913' by William Leech (1881-1968) was commissioned by the National Gallery of Ireland and published in *Lines of Vision: Irish Writers on Art*, edited by Janet McLean (Thames & Hudson, 2014). Several poems from Part Two were included in *Remembering Seamus Heaney* (The Széchenyi Academy of Letters and Arts, Budapest, 2016).

The phrase 'tangled bank' occurs in the last paragraph of Charles Darwin's *On the Origin of Species* (1859). Images and references in 'Bodhidharma Crossing the Blue River on a Reed' are adapted from the work of Joseph Brodsky.

The author is grateful for the helpfulness of the staff at the Issue Desk in the library at Queen's University.